All That Spaz

By: Jamie Aldridge

There is a fool who lives inside all who walk an imperfect existence. What one does because of the fool within, is uncertain based on emotional states. A jolly fool is entertainment, while a blistering fool is unwelcome. To tame your fool, is to learn how to not lose your cool. Forgive yourself for any past, present, or future untamed foolishness. Embrace the foolish part of you that seeks to learn, teach, and love. Dance with the foolish part of you that dreams, laughs, and plays. Part ways with the foolish part of you that steals joy, kills opportunity, and wrecks peace. Once you've accomplished the fool's mission, what's left, is all that wonderful spaz.

Ha, Ha, Ha

Ain't that funny?
Wasn't that hilarious?
How hard did you laugh?
I laughed until I cried!
What the actual…
I might have just peed a little!
Ain't that a trip?
Wasn't that ridiculous?
How much did you believe?
I went along for most of it.
What in the…
I about shit myself!

Family Dinner

Mom was never really there
Dad showed up for the food
Sister ruined brother's mood
Grandpa hardly even moved
Grandma choked on the food
The cousins weren't even invited
Aunt and uncle only brought booze
The dog was the only one enjoying the food
Dessert was when everyone left the table
Next time, let's just eat in our room

It Depends

Maybe
Possibly
Kinda
Perhaps
Eventually
Hopefully
Somewhat
Likely
Percase
Arguably
Conceivable
Plausible

Matrimoney

Contractual agreements don't end well,
both never win even when the other bends
It's not a matter of when it will fail, just how
The differences equal the total distance
between each other's needs
Tears fall under dirty sheets that seemingly smelled clean
Words thrown down the drain of my way is the right way
Criminal vows to keep dying to themselves,
sent their love out of sequential order
Harrowing tales of gun powders covered in layers of bonding blame
Wasted time flew her veil onto the sun-tanned streets
All they needed to do, was never blink

Fun Dips

Sinking ranch is actually bland
Melted cheese gets swarmed by bees
White spinach tastes like prison
Green salsa sours a sandwich's shine
Hummus causes lotus to bloat
Chocolate fondue drips unrelenting caloric dues
Tzatziki whitens the yellowest teeth
Barbecue sauce drops it like it's hot

Blinking Lights

Don't forget what arose from the pit
Warn those who drool over lazy fools
Fight over who's more wrong than right
Hold fast to what they have to lose
Look twice at the message their eyes allude to
Gravitate toward specks of hominy
Wander from lust
Cease to shield yourself from love
Smoke the haze that comes on a cloudy day
Take a good look at who wrote the book
Notice how many lights aren't on
Let the hesitation burn out for goodness' sake

Poop Tents

Saggy pants or wasted space?
You've left plenty of room to go the bathroom in your drawers
When you walk around, it looks like you need an anal vacuum

Loose fit or hidden treasures?
You've created distance to hide what's behind you
When you stand up, it looks like you might drop your inner child

Empty pants or room to grow?
You've failed to rise to the occasion many times
When push comes to shove, it looks like you don't have what it takes

Quality Time

It's about us not you
We are supposedly on a journey together
If we don't connect, it becomes mano a mano
Investing in self is necessary
Prioritizing self is harmless care
If self takes complete precedence, it becomes mano a mano
You can't just do you if you favor my presence
We need to be on the same ride, page, wavelength, and planet
If we aren't even friends, it has become mano a mano

How The Story Grows

When you want it, it shows
When you don't want it, everybody knows

If you can't live without it, you never give up
If you think you'd be better off without it, you eventually lose it

As soon as you remember, they forget
As soon as you lie, the truth comes out

I Love Me

There's one thing that you can't deny
There are two things I'd borrow from you
There are three things we shouldn't do
There are four things that make me scream
There are five things I'll always say
There are six things that keep me up at night
There are seven things I want to see grow
There are eight things that drive me insane
There are nine things I will never eat
There are ten things that repeat in my dreams
There are too many reasons to count

Actually

Babies cry
Toddlers scream
Children stare
Preteens bleed
Teenagers glare
Adults rage
Everyone feels
Someone bites
No one cares

Thank You Jesus

The sun rises and sets
Waters flow
The seas part
Lands feed
Dreamers dream
Losers win
Clouds cry
Plants heal
Trees transform
The wind speaks
All will be revealed

I'll Tell You What

The next time,
he better not make you go all cuckoo
If he doesn't make you say woohoo,
tell him where to stick his poncho

In five years,
he will come unglued
When that happens,
teach him how to line dance

Wasting My Time

I lectured the brick wall into stone
You laughed out loud into a puddle of my good years
I forgave the unforgivable to the point it became excusable
You danced the macarena around my numb feelings
I absorbed every foul word of slander until my bones broke
Your chin rose above prides tipping point
I saw myself vanish into invisible shame particles no one cared about
You paraded your next victim around my deadly desires

Snow Thanks

The ultimate prank is hidden in black ice
The best ride lands you in a snow bank
The softest fall is on white ground
The hardest walk includes steps
The area to avoid is yellow
The worst mistake is forgetting to make pizza with your skis
The biggest laugh arrives in a white ball
The downside is getting stuck
The tricky part is that the avalanche is unpredictable
The good news is that the snow eventually melts

Grandma's Cookie

Stale and old as time
Wrinkled and moisture deplete
Peeing that never ends,
then the drought comes again
Nothing but fake release,
not much hope remains, just a little fear
Not many days excite,
none filled with much surprise, the same old ride again
The sun never shines where cobwebs reside

Stale and old as time
Bitter and oblong
Find a faster ride,
this one always takes too long
Stubborn as her age,
hailing from the south
Wrinkled and moisture deplete
Soured by all the yeast

Say Sorry

One can't forever live free,
to offer absolutely no apologies
No one gets an eternal pass without soothing another's tears
Think of how proud you shouldn't feel
We're all just hanging on for dear life
Stop pretending you don't care
A life best admired is one in which you truly care how others feel

It Doesn't Matter How

You do it, just do it
It doesn't matter how you pay for it,
so long as you pay
It doesn't matter how many shows up,
there's just got to be enough
It doesn't matter how they have it out,
they just need to know
It doesn't matter how you say it,
just that you say it
It doesn't matter how you dress,
just that you look your best
It doesn't matter how you spell it,
the sound is still the same
It doesn't matter how bad it smells,
it still tastes good
It doesn't matter how weird that sounds,
it's a good idea
It doesn't matter how little you think,
the world still blinks
It doesn't matter how happy you are,
the sky will bleed
It doesn't matter how much you care,
free will exists

Goodnight Son

What a privilege it is, to be your mom,
to watch you become a mold,
a mold of the beloved one on the throne

What an honor it is, to impart what I learned,
to use my words to call you up in value

What a wonder it is, to discover what lies inside you,
to listen to music that you make

What a thrill it is, to see you put manners to work,
to laugh when you out humor me

What a pill it is, to know I can't prevent your hurts,
to watch the world around you falling

What a lie it is, to think you can't,
to underestimate what you know

What a love it is, to want to die in your place,
to feel your pain too

What a terror it is, to realize you will make your own nest,
to only be able to say goodnight through text

Could Have Told You So

Hell will never freeze over
Pigs will never fly
The straw will never break the camel's back
Frogs will never be princes
She will never shut up
Time will never stand still
Money will never grow old
Vampires will never suck enough blood
Trash will never take it's self out
Fish will never smell good
Karma will always be a bitch
Christmas will always be merry
Two will always be better than one
Paper will always lose to scissors
Drama will always exist
Gnats will always come and go
Taxes will always be in charge
Sugar will always make you soft
Children will always be a handful
The grass will always be greener

She Did it Again

That girl is the girl we know too well
She cakes on face paint
She wears ultra-revealing clothes
Her lashes are fake
Her mouth is too loud
She drinks tons of rosé
She adorns her finger with nine-inch fake nails
Her tan is far from homemade
Her hair is illegally blonde

That girl doesn't care if you care
She eats caviar for pretentious reasons
She lives to climb social ladders
Her goal is to tell you what to do
Her plot is set in blame

That girl is the pitying type
She sings sorry not sorry all day
She pins the tail on daddy's credit cards
Her family is afraid to speak her truth
Her life exists in vain
That girl will never stop blinding you

Pickled Balls

Neon green and yellow indoor rallies,
Built in holes create a see-through effect,
Soft in practice, but always durable
Easy to spin while never bouncing too high
Often quieter than their players
Lifespan stretches over a couple of rounds
Made in China per usual
Franklins got a good nine-inch stretch
Traveling fast at up to sixty miles per kitchen
Always respecting the no volley rule
Get yours while the plastics not cracked

Political Treason

Every vote that isn't cast counts most
Every vote that is cast counts least
Every uneducated vote cast is irrelevant
Every misinformed vote cast is a waste
Every superficial vote cast is counted twice
Every racially charged vote cast is a positive-negative
Every last-minute vote cast is ignored
Every unsure vote cast is the tie-breaker
Every bribed vote cast tilts the odds
Every forced vote cast muddies the water

Not My Intention

The crime found our address,
but I had no choice except to share my location
The hail found your car,
so it was you who took the wrong turn
The bee stung your highly allergic ass,
yet I told you not to wear that color
The argument escalated,
but it was you who started it

Mugshots Are Forever

Snippity snap
Police are behind you
Blinkity bop
You get pulled over by the cops
Rickity rock
Your body goes into shock
Plippity plop
Now you have to blow and walk
Fickity frock
You wind up in locks
Lickity lock
Your face is permanently clocked

Bring It Back

Mr. Pibb
Elvis
Beanie Babies
Jerry Springer
Chicken Helper
Dollar movies
Laryngitis
Automatic seatbelts
Over the counter decongestant
Discipling children
Written essays
Physical textbooks
Pancho's flan
Modest clothing
Waiting till Christmas
Hairspray in the eyes
Mr. Rogers

Ma Sans Paw

She left, not him
You'll always second guess why
She moved away
You can't believe how far
He stayed right where she left him
She will never go back
He built a new family,
now you don't belong
All because you have a ma and no paw

Frump Roast

Open toed, but covered in socks
Front seat, but no window
Lazy boy, but no recliner
Bottled water, but from the tap
Croissant, but from America
Delivered, but never read
French kiss, but one tongue
Hot dogs, but cool cats
Guns blazing, but zero ammo
Tried and true, but black and blue
White lies, but forgotten truth
Drive thru, but wait in line
Best friends, but they never even listen
Full beard, but a bald head
En route, but nowhere even close
Ripe, but rotten
Sun glasses, but full shade
Take action, but sit back down
About to win, but it's always anyone's race

His Time Was Up

Just as soon as he began to care,
he lost the little dignity he had left
For most of his adult years, he kept to himself
As he approached the end of his existence,
he regretted his reclusive moves
Too little too late became his grave name

Freshly Baked

Couch locked
Snorting seriously
Laughing hysterically
Fighting to stay awake
Undeniable hunger
Carelessly numb
Seeing stars
Ideas flowing from space
Losing will power
Smelling distinctly
Pain dissipating
Making uncommon friends
Wanting to articulate
Leaving them to speculate

Fighting Words

It's all your fault
Go to hell
I wish you would
Try me
His is bigger
Say that one more time

Unhoused Cries

Now I lay me down to beg
I pray the night takes my life
If I die before I heal,
I hope they know I never will

Maybe Baby

We can dive into open blooms of melted cocoa
There will be unholy things to consume if we choose
Sunny days will fade into groomed furry tails of green juniper
All we can eat will stem from
honoring each other's need for pharmalogica

Difficulty roars as we forge through open fields of unsettled hysteria
The digital mafia will tag us to nearby philosophy trees
growing in the sea

Sour sand blows between our two hands
while we sink below what might have been
Air quality unfriends fracturing beliefs,
leaving fate in our father's hands

Trampolina

Sausage extensions all in her hair
Noodles outline her underwear
Beef is glued to her eyelids
Sticks of nuts hang from her ears
Weiner links line her legs
Brats lubricate her ducky lips
Cocky eyes keep her in denial
Pepperoni consumption is stuck in her belly
Ground chuck comes from her butt
Even the smallest shrimp get let in

Yes Way

Sunshine blinds who I am inside
Dark clouds charge my batteries
Nature enlightens my spiritual bank
Heights remind me how he died
Water drowns my worst regrets
Laughter reveals what I really think
Hail makes me finicky
Wind gets the diva parts of me
Fakery boils my enthusiasm
Cold chaps my will to endure
Heat locks the kind side of my mind
Traffic implores me not to forgive

Tattletales

Snitches merely smell dirty dishes instead of washing them
Rats peruse the streets with unverified gossip
Squealers fill up on tea to spill as they please

Canaries sing lyrics posted from beds
Stoolies drop bad news bombs to make their own day
Finks call the police every time a neighbor blinks

Tale bearers walk down aisles,
carrying intellectual property that belongs to others
Yet, the truth will eventually come down unknown chutes

Life Is a Fair

Every day you choose a ride whether you want to or not
Every day you pay an irrevocable price
Every day you wait in some form of a line
Every day you see people wearing masks
Every day you desire unhealthy eats
Every day you meet weird people
Every day you exist in a caged space
Every day you walk on spit
Every day you look for cheap thrills
Every day your life is a living exhibit

Barometers Broken

Pressure rises to the top of your joints,
your bottom jaw slowly begins to drop
The environmental suffocation will never stop
Your ears awaken to a one-two pop
The forecasted front moves in settling hot winds within
Your breath transitions to a state less dense
Suddenly, you can take the altitude in
Your heart swells with rarified circulation
Clouds rest below all your taunting woes
The higher you go, the more mercury rises
Your mind starts to tilt in unrealistic directions
The mercury rises to the top of your blues
Dramatic air fluctuations tighten around your neck like a noose
Down you fall to a climactic bitter end
The ground is left covered with your formerly vigilant broken glass shell

Biggest Loserz

Bullies
Haters
Complainers
Only negative reviewers
Gum droppers
Bed hoppers
Cork breakers
Protein shakers
Fake bacon eaters
Donut thieves
Groundhogs
Widow peakers
Myth busters
Dry humpers
Friends with benefits
Crying dahlias
Evil seekers
Rosé drinkers
Bookmark whores
Loogie leavers
Half-hearted believers
Drunken drivers
Fallen leaves
Money worshippers
Testicle dreamers

Welcome to Hello

It's getting hot in here,
so take off all your nose
We gonna light eyes up,
so that the prime minister knows

Here is where you eat all you can drink
Don't let the door hit you in your toes
You'll find friends that fix your shoes
Set your baggage where the laughter leaks

Hang your coat by the dog's rem sleep
Let loose your will to die for them
Party like it's your very last birthday,
cause we don't care when it really is

It's Time You Learned

How to drive
What to wear
My real name
Who he is
What makes her tick
The secret ingredient
A short cut home
The meaning of friend
Soap matters
Not to do that again
Always buy new
Pairs come in one
They were always rooting for you

Eureka!

Holy spicy bag of Cheetos
Corn roles that last all summer
Bar tops that hold plus sizes
Sail boats that sail without masts
Liver drenched in vomited mayonnaise
Grass stains on face plants
Dads that don't dare look at porn
Moms that don't eat dinner before dinner
Vans unleashing dominoes covered in warranted rage
Sins that stain unseen butt hairs
Love that flies the highest coop
Magnetic basketballs that go in every hoop
Fans that blow farts into your hair
Chins rubbing the bad news in
Pumpkins with rotten seeds, but jolly faces
Oceans of never-ending whale majesty
Trash always going in the trash can
Engineers designing the next city disaster
Skeletons hunting for borrowed clothes
Crayons coloring the day blue

Algorhythm Decisions

It was in my feed
I didn't even have to blink
It read my mind
I didn't think twice
It was more than a subtle proposition
I just couldn't resist
It isn't up for debate
I must cooperate
It knows me best
I no longer think for myself
It tells me what to buy, think, and do
I can't go back in time
It says that won't be fun
I keep eating more cookies
It keeps poaching all my unspoken truths

Candy On My Apple

Tightly bound
Sprinkles all around
Melted sticks of caramel drips
Sticky fingers being blissfully licked
Fiber distribution into the thighs
Smiles resulting in core highs
To the bed they go again
Juices parachuting to their bitter end

Children Who Worry

They turn into nail biting nut jobs and public farting gas mongers
Ten and two rage induced drivers,
who cry when the world has its way,
who laugh when they want to go inane

They let others misspell their name and drop hints that leave zero clues
Obsessive compulsive and empathetic doormats,
who lead instead of following followers
They soak their sins in self sabotaging behaviors

Petty Patrick

He takes cheap shots
He lives below the belt
He blames himself on others
He drowns the truth in hydrogenated oil
He gets drunk on unforgiveness
He wipes his memory with the future
He limps at the sound of shame
He throws stones of lies
He eats salt and vinegar chips then licks your lips
He sings lyrics that don't exist
He will do anything to avoid the short end of the stick
He opens doors to let them close in your face
He sleeps with eyes wide open
He wears shoes that are too big
He smells like oatmeal cooked in the toilet
He knows he is the star of this poem

Global Trouble in Pairs of Dice

When you get more than you bargained for,
delight in the high-stake possibilities
Commiserate with double for your trouble rollers
See the numbers turn in your favor
Five of a kind of days are always on the horizon
Black and white landings will yield lucky colored stairs to VIP tables
Sit back patiently while the political deck is shuffled
Pick the card that flatters your dice
Go all in even against a best friend
Two ones hit the table like eyes calling your bluff

I Don't Know Why

People steal
People kill
People destroy
People lie
People die
People spy
People poop
People stoop
People shoot
People fight
People connive
People rape
People save
People hope
People laugh
People sing
People smile
People give
People forgive
People hug
People pray
People help
People share
People love

Could Have Fooled Me

The game already ended
The food got eaten
The rain stopped
The phone died
The car kept driving
The squirrel got away
The ball was dropped
The tears dried up
The gift kept giving
The trash took itself out
The glass was always full
The road never ends
The gate is always open
The picture was edited
The sun keeps shining

Poets

They don't know it, they grow it
They don't show it, they speak it
They don't fake it, they feel it
They don't borrow it, they own it
They don't cry about it, they fight it
They don't please with it, they just do it
They don't flex it, they hide in it
They don't bite at it, they chomp at it
They don't wash it; they keep wearing it
They don't wait on it, they sit on it
They don't suggest it, they recommend it
They don't govern it, they release it
They don't waste it, they use it
They don't second guess it, they accept it
They don't just say it, they spray it

Mugshots

Shame frozen in time forever
Real exposure rising high
Debts dying in the night of day
Peace leaving the prince in power
Karma kicking the kites to the ground
Sin seeds sailing on bars of steel
Life lessons lost on stolen lemonade
Heroes hovering hell flames
Thousands of tyrants telling truths
Generational gut games lost
Beasts breaking down brilliant minds
Potential for present positive predictions
Fear swallowed fast and furiously
Cost of dying calling crime complete
Pixels that forever bleed

Bath And Body Cheese

You taste more than simply macabre
I always wondered why your junk can be nasal identified from the street
Your mom must have slabbed her pregnant belly
with leftover swine grease

It was never ok with your sponge, to create nonmalignant tile film
Is there something we could do, to spare shoes from your feet?

Love is blind, but it possesses all other senses
Please be so kind, as to undo bridges that take us to your rankest places

Everyone understands why you're still single
Hope can be found in willing and brave botanicals
For now, we'll label your scent: trash can tears

Silent Nights

Home alone
Only got my phone
What will I do?

People talk to me through the screen
They don't know why I'm listening
What will I say?

My eyes are fixed on never ending reels
My mind is becoming theirs
What will they think?

Sicko-Dicko

Say the worst possible thing
Kick them while they're down
Poke fun instead of showing love
Fire the ones doing good business
Take away desire to smile and keep on living
Lust for whom you give the middle finger
Never offer them an ounce of healthy liver
Creep around to steal their mental spoils
Drag their pain around in a see-through punching bag
Break their heart into black and white comic strips

Vows

You say yes
I say no
Who holds the end of the hose?
I will forgive
You will endure
They will never believe
We will always wish
Death will inevitably impart,
distance from each other's heart

He Doesn't Care

He never did
He never will
He always won't
He always lies

He sometimes tries
He sometimes denies
He rarely gives
He rarely archives

Nutsicles

You will know them by their frozen fruit
They refuse to melt into reality's cup
We do business with their leash wearing brains
They are self-captured pubescent plants
When they move, the wind hollows their groves
If you shoot them straight, they ooze toxicant
As the wind blows, they fall onto chins
Have pity on them, because they eat lowly hooves

Break A Leg

Good luck my dear
Best wishes old friend
You got this sister
Win big homie
Show em who's boss brother
Make them think twice partner
Give em hell pal
Take home the cake big momma
Losing is not an option mejo
Finish what they started bruh
The world's your oyster big pappa
Sock it to them you sassy beotch
Leave nothing on the table sailor
Sink your heels all the way in buddy
Pull those big girl panties up girlfriend
Knock em dead lover
Win big or go home player
Leave no box unchecked hot stuff
Only the best sit here mister
Yo, just believe in yourself

Keep Dancing

The music skips sometimes
The music might even come to a sudden stop

Don't let your pas de bourrée drop
Don't forget how to execute hip hop

The audience is tied between laughs and claps
The audience doesn't know how hard you've worked

Don't drink in what they aren't afraid to say
Don't allow their fear to run you off stage

The body slowly depletes of its jazz
The body won't always remember the steps

Don't feel limited by what's within your stretch
Don't stop tapping to the essence of your own choreography

Gravy Trainz

Crash into cash money
Live high on the heaviest hog
See silver and gold as it goes down their throats
Talk over the toots of their green horn
Breath in the fumes of flowing money trails
Cry while they blink and more dollars grow on their trees
Smell the iron right off of where you will never go
Wash your face in water they already used
Lean against their wall of unpaid dues
Trip over the currency legacy never left to you

Jesus Juice

It's what you need, so find a humble bended knee
It's how he lives through you,
so let your cup run over for the world to drink

It's worth unending hallelujahs
It's our reason for being, so jump for joy,
even when no one else is dancing to the music

It's the salt in your water
It's the only healthy addiction,
so start consuming at an early age

It's the purpose driving your why
It's the reason the devil lies,
so don't ever believe you have no true divine calling

It holds the power to help you rebuke
It cleanses iniquity causing confusion,
so be grateful in every season

Insta Delight

Slam the door on their ugly crying face
Laugh at what you didn't say
Drive right past memory lanes
Mow the lawn at dusk in a skirt
Hang up when both have said goodbye twice
Cross the line after checking them nicely
Wash your hands with non-alcoholic beer
Delete the evidence when you eat happily
Grow in empathy when they lose the bet
Make sure your crotch knows it's ethnicity

Bathroom Wars

Mines cleaner than yours
Mines smells better than yours
Mines bigger than yours
Mines has nice toilet paper
Mines has recycled toilet water
Mines makes sure you can see everything
Mines drunk on pink
Mines keeps your secrets
Mines a good place to meditate
Mines where dead people levitate
Mines full of self-denial
Mines full of animal wallpaper
Mines got the perfect amount of shallow lighting
Mines only takes a few tries to flush my bull shit
Mines makes you want to lose weight
Mines shows you the house will never really be clean
Mines forgives you when you fart
Mines shoots arrows at your prideful heart
Mines is open every time you need it
Mines is for guests
Mines is for everyone

Swimsuits

You wear them,
but would really rather not
You blame them,
but it's not their fault

You laugh at them,
but the joke is on you
You use them to impress,
but your efforts are too obvious

You pick the one that isn't right for you,
but everyone's afraid to tell you the truth
You like how they look in theirs,
but your heart is ten times better than theirs
You don't even get in all the way,
but insist that you're a water child

You make the smallest splash,
but you urinate in the pool
You make the biggest splash,
but no one cares when you drown

Not At All

His feet are too small
Her butt is too flat
His career is going nowhere
Her mouth moves indirectly
His jokes are offensive
Her food tastes regifted
His game smells like yesterday
Her friends drink too much
His arms are more developed than his legs
Her mom is two faced
His dad has a beer gut
Her I.Q. embarrasses the dog
His lisp is less than crisp
Her hair holds ten years old lies
His balls literally forgot to drop
Her favorite songs are about death
His secret tune is I love Henry

Laps

Back and forth with minimal breathing
Over and under waters not worth believing
Aquatic tremors of wishful thinking
Shallow dreams sinking all the deeper
Dolphin rides that disturb mythical speakers
Butterflies drowning in shocking numbers
Breaststrokes lacking genuine cleavage
Goggles disclosing disjointed fears
Backstrokes into walls of poised shame
Inhales of unknowing sins
Staying under just for attention
Body weights found irrelevant
Only jaws knows when the race ends

Drink Less

Abnormality
Adversity
Absurdity
Admissibility
Acidity
Accidentality
Accessibility
Aboriginality
Alternativity
Ambiguity
Amnesty
Answer ability
Animosity
Annuity
Artificiality
Audacity
Authority
Autoimmunity
Avoidability
Anxiety

Prime

Real estate
Numbers
Rib
Player
Years
Animals
Instincts
State
Land
Minister
Time

Hair

Spray
Strand
Day
Piece
Brush
Extension
Dryer
Loss
Color
Tie
Bow
Length
Trends
Gel
Net
Follicle

Sounds

Alright
Fine
Bad
Great
Kosher
Plausible
Loud
Brilliant
Gay
Whack
Lame
True
Magical
Perfect
Tragic
Fake
Bitchy
Reasonable
Problematic
Risky
Expensive
Ridiculous
Outrageous
Contagious
Lavish
Weird
Peculiar
Fishy
Suspect
Fair
Sublime

Proverbs For Tomorrow

Climb down from your wall
See that your heart needs patience to grow
Hold minds with hopeful souls
Cry money into richly soiled land
Dash around thorns and bitter stones
Chase only what's east of Eden
Know how to recover what fear steals
Trickle crumbs of love to sour blokes
Shake the hand of every green thumb
Eat cake to celebrate honest victories
Promise to never forget the start
Make sure you laugh to the finish

Main Squeeze

Above all other members of faculty,
but still beneath the King of Kings
Most likely to rope all my cattle,
but least likely to chase other tails

Caretaker of my insecurities,
but lovingly honest about time to kill
Provider of smiles that erase internal frowns,
but nowhere near rings of financial disaster

Bumper Butts

Pale cheeks squeaking on one another at night
Dark holes dare to toss their coronary fund salad
Bright lights shine mischievously on backwards spoons of pride
Shadows grow in cracks splitting empty assets from both sides
Flashes of unreachable hair come into bottom vision
Twinkling beams rise above rounding odors of unrelenting contemplation
Glimmers of hate clash with sagging cushions for life
Afterglows of remorse release from all the backwards decisions

Poop Words

Nothing smells as bad as what comes out of your mouth
Fertilized dirt is more precious than anything you have to say
The stench your mouth creates lasts for decades
Those on the receiving end, are left with an unflushable taste
Your thoughts integrate with what Satan ate
By the time your inner vile digests,
you have come up with eviler to say

Towels For Days

Curled fingers gripping white
Some wet, some stained,
some clean, some dirty,
some new, some used

The dirty are tossed into soapy sauce
All twist, all turn,
all absorb, all crinkle
all connect, all spin

Out they come smelling like new
Some stick, some drip,
some drop, some refuse
some hide, some separate

In they go to the fiery den
All suffocate, all cry
all suffer, all fall
all surrender, all die

More are made until the timer ends

Stanley Cuffs

All the empty cups are on display, on display
Empty cups are the most expensive, most expensive
Full cups realize the big decision, big decision
Empty cups make sure you see them, see them
Full cups need no external recognition, external recognition
Empty cups get left behind, left behind
Full cups know how to break free, break free
Empty cups believe there is no other way, other way

Simon Says

Stay away from hoes
Keep the lint out of your toes
Think faster than trees can
Drink every last drop like a real man
Press no, then swipe right
Be more perceptive than the goats
Offer prayers for good hearted nihilists
Pull the lion's tail twice
Jump sideways to avoid trouble
Tell your darkest secret to release karma from its mission

Manpons

Common sense goes in one hole,
and then in between the other hole

Stories are told by one linguist,
and then sold to interpreters of choice

Drama creeps out of unspeakable crevices,
and then dries up the root of every chest hair

Solidarity fumigates swamp like moisture,
and then ropes in more selfish vulgarity

Crisis erupts from the tip of the top,
and then stabilizes at the edge of homebase

Nightmares leap back and forth from cheeks,
and then land where leaks are sleeping

Bent Stick Energy

He's hung from his own noose
He's obviously been with a moose
He's clearly more than confused
He's out of lives
He's told too many lies
He's subject to weird lower body high fives
He's swarming in mental fleas
He's not worth bended knees
He's run out of boyish charm
He's poked too many pairs of thighs
He's treating them how he feels
He's got no one left on his side

The One

He knows you best
He lived before you
He fell on your sword
He'd do it again
He needs your voice as much as you need his
He lives for your sake
He pays for you
He expects love in return
He bleeds the most
He waits for you
He hopes you don't lose hope
He will never abandon you
He dries your tears
He silences your fears
He can't wait till you need him
He loves you more

Effing Hangry

Ravenous
Delirious
Relentless
Dangerous
Ridiculous
Dreadful
Resentful
Dramatic
Reprehensible
Desperate
Rude
Defiant

Doors Open

Welcome to my humble heart
May only divine destiny do us part
The future looks far brighter, so tally-ho
Only good things are in store

Golden opportunity awaits
Refuse to accept any lesser fate
Embrace the light of each new day
Pay respect to lessons learned along the way
Thankfully, faith has brought you here to stay

Doors Closed

Stay away
There's no more possibility
What could have been,
will never ever be
About face

Go find your proper space
The bar has been forever raised
All our days will soon be erased
Let's forget each other's names
Unfortunately, we're both to blame

Filter, Filter on The Wall

Who's the fakest of them all?
How do we know who they really are?
Which face does their name disgrace?
Is that nose auto generated?
Are they really capable of touching their toes?
Will they always look that way?
When will they own who they aren't?
Shall I just learn to accept them as a work of pretend art?

The Right Brew

How pale you are
How light you are
How fruity you are
How versatile you are
How bitter you are
How aromatic you are
How bright you are
How smooth you are
How balanced you are
How perfectly malty you are
How refreshing you are
How crisp you are
How strong you are
How chill you are
How hoppy you are
How happy you make me
How silly you make me
How blurry you make them
How friendly you make us

Tears Are in The Air

Take a step toward love
Trip over what they didn't say
Toss your fear up to the clouds
Turn where it doesn't hurt
Try to run your fastest
Tuck in your tolerant tongue
Trace their pace in your face
Tell your feelings to the wind
Travel as far as your feet can land
Tempt your nose to smell the truth
Taste the pain that failed to grow

In My Dreams

You aren't you
We can all twerk
I never met any jerks
Hair never changes
We die in our sleep
Love never fades
Tempers never flare
Babies don't blankly stare
Animals roam free
Feet don't stink
Clowns possess tans
The poop never hits the fan
School is actually fun
No one is allowed to drive dumb
Suicide is not a thing

In Your Dreams

They're always sweet
Football makes you complete
Everyone's words kiss your feet
The sun cures your fears
Dog's drool enough to fill an entire pool
Flames flare when eagles soar
No one thinks very deep
Secrets live beneath green trees
Women pay for themself
Finger nails are trimmed in the wild
Sliders always make it to home base
Lovers don't need to exchange names
Age is a number that means not a thing
White never shows your mistakes
The choice is always yours

Taco Poison

Place the heart of the matter in a shell
Throw some careless on it
Sprinkle some disease on top
Cover it with a white creamy muzzle
Drop a few drops of blood on the cream
Take a sneaky corner bite when they least expect it
Allow secrets to ooze out of the hard shell
Lick your fingers to death

Fine Then

Sons of bitches let their pants sag
Ignorant people use his name in vain
Fathers and mothers refuse to get along
Rosemary only gets eaten seasonally
People pick their nose in public
Dogs drool, but are wiser than most tools
Hair grows back with a vengeance
Trauma and pride explosively collide
Pop tarts are for everyone
Salad is harder to eat dry
Hidden talent goes undiscovered
Vegetables don't eat themself
All good fruit is capable of rotting
Pizza comes with too many options
Unwanted items are the ones on sale
Three is a crowd
Jail is way worse than school
Only time will tell
No one is ever truly happy
No one is ever their real self

To This, I Say No

Brown nosing your way
Wearing just to impress
Seafood towers
Two faces
One right way
Cheese for days
Shooting blanks
Not enough toothpaste
My name in the enemy's mouth
Floating in the middle of the ocean
Big pieces of steak
Too much on my plate
Pimples on the cheeks
Wine that smells like an egg
Never knowing what to do
Nose hairs on the outs
Adults in daisy dukes
Two balls in one hoop
Cars that smell like puke
Rooms with no windows
Matches with short sticks

To This, I Say Yes

Vodka with no taste
Doing right behind the scenes
Growing up even when it hurts
Less sugar in my veins
Finding out it was just a mistake
Loving the insane
Showing time who's the boss
Wiping the slate clean
Leaving the past in the past
Making coffee disappear
Driving past bleak space
Taking baths by myself
Breaking ground on seeds of shame
Watching just for laughs
Animals responding to their names
Being quiet in a storm
Sending love to those in pain
Giving up being right
Eliminating the rest of the problem
Consuming a rightful consequence
Letting them die first
The thought of never getting fat

Halftime

Potty breaks
Incidental napping
Liquid refills
Temperamental chatter
Bet on what you want to have happen
Handfuls of salty cadavers

Purple Ant Eaters

Oh, how they come marching in, marching in
They crush what took ten million to build
You fight and bite with all your might
Thousands run at the sight of them
Many are fast, but few survive
All you want is to defend your column
Eating you alive is worth their points of view
Their noses are long because they live to lie to themselves daily
There is power in numbers, but more and more live in rebellion
Your crew burns with fire for truth
Their crew grows more dysfunctional each day
Tolerating their intolerant ways won't do
They must eat every last one of you
Keep piling your piles of truth
Maybe one day, they will realize they actually like the taste of truth

It's About Time You Knew

I love you
I really, really do
I need you
I don't want to go without you
I see you
I won't leave you
I hear you
What you say lingers
No one else makes sense
We can't erase it

Karen's Closet

Ten million pickleball skirts
Migraine inducing floral scents of gossip
Pearl necklaces attained despite brown bag special status
High heels of uneducated judgement
Cotton scarves picked after closing time
Belts with holes of intentional deceit
Garden hats that bruise annual flowers
Coats that zip up what really matters
Dresses to seduce forgettable laughter
Pants worn to drive your car faster
Shirts advertising rosé drinking instructions
Gloves to choke the smiles off their faces

Where The Sun Doesn't Shine

Your anus
My anus
Their anus
Subcutaneous fat
Scalps covered by a cap
Unvisited places on the map
Hearts covered in secondary shame
Individuals enslaved to seeking secular fame
First names created after the birth certificate
Artificial intelligence used for evil

Where The Sun Shines

Sidewalk crevices grow unexplained statuses
Grass pastures allow big disasters
Fence holes make the best binoculars
Ant piles house all the people's secrets
Rooftops cover all the inside bruises
Bleachers are where they go for no reason
The water's edge drools leftover sangria
Tree tops seal the wounds from last season

Particles

Time creates dents in the mind,
damage that requires unknown amounts of space to reverse
Black matter creeps into the unkept mental spaces,
causing wisdom to separate from truth

Pieces of forgotten memory form
What remains are loose cannons of unoriginal recollections of reality
Nerves disconnect at the root stem,
turning out the lights on formidable dreams

Eyes That Can't See

Blink, blink, think
Blink, blink, drink
Blink, blink, sink
Blink, blink, dream
Blink, blink, downstream
Blink, blink, scream
Blink, blink, find
Blink, blink, overkind
Blink, blink, blind
Blink, blink, ignore
Blink, blink, snore
Blink, blink, score

Wake Up Sister

You are beneath his ego
You are his verbal punching bag
You are his last thought
You are a living breathing joke to him
You are less than a blow-up doll in his opinion
You are not more important than the game

Your feelings are irrelevant to him
Your perspective is the trash in the can
Your earnings are pennies in his eyes
Your beauty means nothing at the end of the day
Your brains are his to bash
Your heart is his property to crush

This collection of poems is dedicated to all individuals who don't think before they speak.

www.ingramcontent.com/pod-product-compliance
Lightning Source LLC
Chambersburg PA
CBHW050654160426
43194CB00010B/1941